The Bonds We Keep

Poems by
Karin Hoffecker

BLUE LIGHT PRESS ◆ 1ST WORLD PUBLISHING

1ST WORLD
PUBLISHING

SAN FRANCISCO ◆ FAIRFIELD ◆ DELHI

The Bonds We Keep

BLUE LIGHT PRESS
www.bluelightpress.com
bluelightpress@aol.com

1ST WORLD PUBLISHING
PO Box 2211
Fairfield, IA 52556
www.1stworldpublishing.com

BOOK & COVER DESIGN
Melanie Gendron
melaniegendron999@gmail.com

AUTHOR PHOTO
Steve Bartley

COVER ART
Margaret Nieman

FIRST EDITION

ISBN: 978-1-4218-3718-5

For my mother and father
and for my son Kyle.

Acknowledgments

My gratitude to the editors of the following journals and anthologies for first publishing these poems, some in slightly different versions.

The Comstock Review, Geometry Lessons

Gathering Flowers: Living, This is Us

with the Death of a Child, Home Again

The MacGuffin, Crossing Over, Fascinators, These Days

The Metro Times, For Buzzy

Peninsula Poets, This is Us

Penumbra, Mrs. Davis' Chair

Special thanks to Blue Light Press and to Diane Frank and Melanie Gendron for their sound advice and support. My gratitude to the Southeast Michigan Poetry Meetup Group. Carla Dodd, David Fitch, Marie Davids, Eric Greene, Nina Robb, and Dana Newhouse. Many thanks to Edward Haworth Hoeppner for his wise and generous counsel.

Contents

Mrs. Davis' Chair

For Nana (1906-2001)

Two months since the funeral,
when early March sun
in liquid rays coaxed crocuses,
forsythia barely buds,
too early even for the pansy's
painted face. At the festival,
I remember times we wandered
the park, you dismayed
at *the things called art today.*
I find the photographs,
the antique garden chair
armless yet elegant,
its curved back, sturdy scrolled
legs, a woven white iron seat.

The artist tells me the story –
finding his neighbor's vintage
yard chair, borrowing it for the day.
Taking it to the bleached sands
of a North Carolina beach
to photograph in dawn's
fiery light. On her 98th birthday,
he gave her the picture –
Mrs. Davis' Chair at the Beach.
In return, she gave him the chair.
When she passed at 102, he took
the chair to photograph. Capturing
scenic vistas in all fifty states.

I flip through the pictures, notice
the slant of light, snippets of time,

places traveled . . . . *Mrs. Davis'*
Chair Overlooking Lake Isabella,
Mrs. Davis' Chair Beside the Mackinac
Bridge, Mrs. Davis' Chair at Sunset,
on a porch with hydrangeas, under
a weeping willow. I choose
Mrs. Davis' Chair in a Field of Wild
Flowers, nestled in a floral sea
of Michigan's lavender and green.
A photograph you would love.

Fascinators

After Hats by Philip Treacy

At the art museum that summer,
his hats were center stage. Cased
in Plexiglas boxes, each a sculpture
of exquisite beauty. A black beret
adorned with military buttons,
quail feathers curled like question
marks. The stunning silver mesh
saucer, its fanciful bow taking flight.

Now the Duchess of Cambridge,
her modern take on hats makes
headlines. Sophistication of a navy
taffeta pillbox, its diamond-cut
feathers. The whimsy of a crimson
headpiece, single floral bud sprouting
from a bed of ruby mesh, stunning
against the sheen of her auburn hair.

You, daughter-in-law, not British
royalty, but another whose style
dazzles. Your handbags and shoes
fashion forward. A Kate Spade satchel,
of ostrich-embossed cowhide in fresh
green. The peep-toe olive green heels
with jeweled bows you wore on your
wedding day. Your fascinator, a flower
of silk chiffon, bird-cage netting, layers
of hand-stitched fabric petals.

And that September afternoon in 1959,
another wedding. I find the photograph
tinted with age, other keepsakes: my

aunt's handmade note cards of dried
wild flowers, the bronze giraffe she loved.
I see her in a simple ivory dress, vintage
beige velvet headband, its veil of delicate
lace soft against her face. Her fascinator
I treasure, now that she is gone. I try
it on, see her smile in mine. Remember,
the weight of her embrace.

Brooches

For My Mother

The brooch is making a comeback,
this year's hottest accessory.

I think of Bertoia's brooches
at the museum. Ornamental
centipede in hammered brass;
a spider web spun in silver thread.

I remember my first jewelry,
not a brooch, but a stickpin.

The rose gold flower, its pin
the stem. And the twin crescent
moons I wore on soft sweaters.

I remember my mother's
brooches. The antique jewel
from England. A gilt mesh basket
holding pearl and ruby blooms.

The diamond and sapphire gem
she wore at her grandson's
wedding. But it's her diamond
wreath brooch, its elegance I covet.

Oh, to wear it on a little black dress.
Glittering leaves catching the light.

Crossing Over

For Jane (1930-2009)

I've tucked your cards away for safe
keeping, fewer notes the last year.
Now talismans to all you adored:
an orchid bud, the hummingbird,
a sleeping fawn. I see your familiar
hand, feel the comfort of your script.

I remember when you let go, a wintry
March night after cancer won. *Let the*
light of late afternoon shine through
chinks in the barn. How you loved
the poetry of Jane Kenyon. I grieved
never talking about books with you again.

Never sipping lattes on your wooden
deck overlooking the bay, or visiting
your gardens awash in color: clusters
of pink hollyhocks, burgundy petunias,
potted red geraniums you cared for even
when chemo left you too weak to garden.

The clairvoyant I visit said the spirit
world is powerful, those who've crossed
over still among us. The same day, I find
a book of poetry you'd given me fallen
from the shelf. I pick it up, see its title:
Here from Away.

For Buzzy

(October 1956 – April 1963)

This autumn afternoon,
red and gold fire in the canvas
of the sky. I remember Easter
Sunday, 1960. My brother,
dressed in gray flannel
trousers, jacket, boxy bow tie.
We smiled hand-in-hand,
my white crocheted gloves,
a ruffle at the wrist.

I remember the world
as it used to be, birthday
parties, crepe paper streamers,
chocolate cake, and you
in pointed cardboard hat,
pastel blower pressed between
your lips. Halloween you dressed
as a sheriff, straw cowboy hat,
black leather boots, shiny silver
star pinned to your chest.

On Good Friday the world
turned black, smoke billowing,
when match flame ignited
too quickly the yellow straw
of the doghouse bed, you inside.
My secret guilt for the times
I screamed, *I wish you were dead.*

Guilt in knowing you took
the long-stemmed kitchen
matches, the ones with the bright

cherry colored heads. Later,
the stench in mother's clothes
and hair, the odor I still smell
when fall fireplaces glow.

After the funeral, return
to life without you – my
second grade classmates
suddenly friendly, invite
me to play kick ball, make
room for me at the cafeteria
table. My teacher wearing
stilettos and a tight skirt,
hugging me too close,
telling me *to be brave*.

And for months after,
your room left untouched.
Your scent lingering on bed
sheets, your cap guns
and holster, the planet playset
with space men and rockets.
Your dirty canvas tennis shoes,
left forgotten in the closet.

A photo arrives in the mail,
a glossy black and white.
My cousin's son and daughter
posed arm-in-arm in tap shoes.
Startled by the likeness, same
tousled hair, spray of freckles,
same impish grin dressing
his face. I trace your smile.
Stop time.

The Blessing

For Margaret (1928-2013)

To know again that April
is the cruelest month –
you passing on a moonlit
late April evening. Your death
not unexpected, but the news
sudden. I hear the words
heart failure, and you are gone.
Now, I sit reminiscing about
our long history. You caring
for my toddler son when I was
too ill to be his mother,
too depressed to leave my bed.
It gave me comfort knowing
he was safe and loved.

I remember when you needed
me. How the dizziness
frightened you. No longer able
to leave your home. The life
you made in simple things:
television talk shows, books,
computer games. The times
I visited and brought the Oriental
chicken salad you loved.
The haircuts I didn't know
I could give, you reminding
me: *Don't cut my bangs too short.*

Days after the first Christmas
without you, I'm watching
Call the Midwife on PBS.

I think of how we loved talking
about the London midwives
of the 1950s. I want to call,
to tell you what a blessing
you were in my life. The place
in my heart I hold for you.

Farewell Reading

For Edward Haworth Hoeppner

It was your farewell reading,
that damp misty November
evening. You said Stevens
would call a "frozen-in-limbo"
kind of night. And I'm here
to celebrate and remember.

You say you loved teaching.
A career spanning twenty-seven
years, where you traveled
from Minnesota to Alabama.

The years in the south, blistering
heat and storm-filled skies.
Foreign to the cool, sun-dappled
woods of Rochester, Michigan.

Now, this is where you start
your day with a walk. Then sit
before a blank computer screen.
You wondering if you're done,
nothing more to say at sixty-four.

But when you read your new work,
about the places you've hidden –
Behind my eyelids. Under covers.
Never in the mirror very well –
I know you have more words to draft.

Between poems, you chat about
your love of the old Olivetti
typewriter you carried on your

back. In the early years, how you were
soothed by the clacking of keys,
the bright ping of the return bar.

Your dislike of pencils,
the scratchy marking of paper
an angry assault to your ears.
Your love of Rumi, Wallace
Stevens and how you still
read Emily Dickinson every day.

On my drive home, I think
about what your students will
miss. You, walking into class
in blue jeans, denim shirt, wool
tie. Shoes worn without socks,
and the battered brown leather
briefcase you still carry today.

Settling in, perched on desk's
edge, you begin with Stevens:

Out of this same light, out of
the central mind, we make
a dwelling in the evening air,
in which being there is enough.

For Magdalena

How you huddled over books in the college
library, looking for Renoir's *Seated Bather*.
You admired the painting at the museum,
the pink blush of her shimmering skin.
As my student you learned the language,
the history of this country. Where freedom,
like the soft swell of the bather's flesh,
is ample. You gave me a statue of Rodin's
Thinker the first Christmas. The next year,
you wrapped an apricot scarf around my neck
saying, *This gives you such color.*

At the coffeehouse with lattes and fruit muffins,
we talked about Tarik, the Pakistani boyfriend
you moved in with your first months here.
About his demands that you learn to cook *basmati*,
aromatic rice of his homeland, clean his family's
cramped flat, communicate with his mother who
spoke no English. Forced to entertain his friends
when your heart preferred school, books a sanctuary.
You stopped calling and I walked the college
halls missing you.

In late fall you return, hair knotted at the neck.
Oversized sweater covering your hips, belly bulging
beneath. Hug tentative when you say, *I thought
you would be angry.* I place my hands on the contour
of your unborn child. Your absence palpable.
A month later I visit with gifts: almond coffeecake,
diapers, *Goodnight Moon*, a blue blanket. Small
comforts for your new life. You sit nursing your son
Mustafa, the chosen one, the name Tarik insisted
on. You say, *He wanted me to shave his head for luck.*
I stroke the fine black silk.

Geometry Lessons

For Maryanne (1955-2000)

You tutored me in tenth grade
geometry to a D. Long afternoons
smoking Benson & Hedges,
discussing the mystery
of teenage boys. Only minutes
spent on classification of angles,
properties of parallel lines.

And always, your mother
in black beret and ballet slippers
spinning perfect pirouettes
across the kitchen floor.
Everywhere, piles of pink tutus,
recital music, magazines. Odd
comfort housed in the bits of clutter.

Thirty years later, your death,
an accident off the Greek Isles –
swallowed by crystal-lipped seas,
your body a starfish washed ashore,
strands of seaweed in your hair.

No shape for death so sudden,
grieving daughters still girls
in satin hair ribbons, cotton
socks cuffed in lace. No mother
to explain the angles of the sun.

Home Again

For Kyle

I am waking my dog in front
of our first home and I think
of you. I would like to step inside
this house, one more time. If only
to hold close that boy you were.

You, with a broken leg at two,
singing to Sesame Street. You,
sprawled on the floor, with
the Fisher-Price farm you loved.

I remember the birthday parties,
homemade cakes, gift bags,
and shiny balloons. Your third
birthday with a circus theme.

You, hiding in your bedroom,
frightened of the man with the red
clown nose, and brown floppy shoes.

I see you and the boy from next
door, with construction helmets,
riding bright yellow bulldozers
up and down the driveway.

We visit the park, your joy in simple
things: swings, the slide, a sand box.
The place I take your daughter now
to remember you. The son and father
I mourn, leaving home too soon.

Expiration Date

For Dr. Brian Connolly

I think of all the years I sat each week,
on your leather couch, raw and vulnerable,
unpacking my life story. The secrets,
the shame, the soul-crushing sorrow.
How you helped me through a tunnel
of malaise, into a light-filled world.

I'm climbing the two flights of stairs
to your office one last time.
Three decades of our working together
have reached their expiration date,
as you embrace well-earned retirement.

You apologize for this being another
loss after a lifetime of grief and suffering.
My beloved brother's tragic death in a fire
he set playing with matches. Abandoned
by parents drunk with unimaginable sorrow.

And the day I learned my beautiful boy
had passed away at thirty-four, I climbed
those stairs, my heart shattered. The loss
I feared most in life happening. Now, my
mother's aging, her swift decline ignites
my sadness. I watch her ebb away.

On this frigid January afternoon, we say
our goodbyes. You suggest we'll see each
other in the neighborhood. And when our paths
cross, the words of Rumi will remind me
of our time together. The gratitude I have
for walking this journey with you.

The dark thought, the shame, the malice, meet
them at the door laughing, and invite them in.
Be grateful for whatever comes, because each
has been sent as a guide from beyond.

Now That You Are Gone

This month of unseasonable November,
I walk to remember the summer sun,
long days of light, before the winter
grays descend, slick ice-covered paths
I must navigate.

The sidewalks, where last week I found
a ten dollar bill. I put it in my pocket.
Perhaps some chocolate, flowers, tea,
with this unexpected fortune.

Days later, I discover the children's
book for my granddaughter. Thrilled
to find it in the park's lending library,
the owl shaped box of treasures.

On other walks, a small silver bracelet
hanging on an evergreen bush. A few
blocks more, a dead baby mouse.
Its gray, velvety fur curled like a comma.

Beside the construction site, a single
lavender wool glove without a mate.
Grim reminder of the endless season
of grief that awaits in winter.

Today, the week before Thanksgiving,
a record 73 degrees. I walk to the lake
and others are there too. Families taking
photos, fishing, tossing a football.

In front of the waterfall, long-stemmed
red roses and petals scattered. I think
of you son, so like the flowers, blooming
in life. You are gone eight months.
Never forgotten. Like roses in November.

The Bonds We Keep

For Kyle (1981-2016)

A cold, gray, slushy February day –
and I remember two years ago,
you driving across country with Syed.
Excitement about your new job
in California. I look at your Instagram
photos, the captions so you: #14mpg,
#X5M is a road beast, #no tickets,
#5 casinos, #roll tide. I text the memory
to Syed, who is remembering this trip too.

The enduring history you had as friends,
on and off the road. He tells me about
this year's Gold Rush road rally in June.
Its course: Boston, Detroit, Las Vegas,
Tucson. I will send some of your ashes
with him to spread. All places you lived
and loved.

The anniversary of your death next month,
and I hold close the pictures of our life
in every room. On table tops, the ceramic
bowls you made. The watercolor painting
you brought home rolled up in your
backpack. Your favorite t-shirt folded,
lying on an afghan at the end of my bed.

Videos on my phone of you and Nell,
your daughter's laughter ringing in my ears.
A memorial fund I start at your high school.
Remembering your passion for sports,
the years of football, wrestling, lacrosse.
The candle I burn when the days are too long,
too dark missing you.

This is Us

I send some of your ashes to Las Vegas
with Syed, your best friend, in a bag
that held my first iPod. The one you gave
me as a gift on my 50th birthday,
with the music I loved: Depeche Mode,

R.E.M., Coldplay. The Replacements
singing, *The ones we love best are*
the ones we lay to rest. How you loved
me deeply in your thirty-four years.

The pumpkin you surprised me with,
carving out the letters REM, our dance
to Nightswimming at your wedding.
The photo you took outside a German
stadium. The band's handprints in cement.

I think of you, spreading your ashes
beneath the evergreen tree in the backyard.
The sapling we planted when you were
in grade school. How you marveled
at its height when you came home to visit.

I treasure our years together. At the lake,
boating, swimming, a July wedding
by the shore. Memories impossible
to forget. In these indigo waters you loved,
your ashes swirl like wings opening.

In Memoriam

For Kyle, Senior Awards Night (May 31, 2018)

The words Maple Field, large maroon
letters on the stadium wall, take me back.
Your high school years at Seaholm,
rich in opportunity and reward.

Nights I sat shivering on the bleachers,
watching with pride. You, mud-stained
and sweaty, tackling crosstown
opponents on the football field.

It was your fierce loyalty to your friends,
forged on Maple Field, I remember
most. Friendships begun in grade school,
on playgrounds and baseball diamonds,
still in high school.

Steadfast teammates and companions,
until you passed. Those you called
daily and visited, even living miles
apart. Friends who were your brothers.

Gone two years now, I start a Memorial
Award in your name. I visit the wall
of honor at Seaholm, look for the maroon
tiles with the maple leaf: *Three Generations
KN 52, KH 73, KTH 2000.* Grandmother,
mother, son. Our legacy etched in stone.

The Lunch

For Jamie

It's been two years and the struggle
is real for both of us, who loved
you most. How, as wife and mother,
we navigate grief in different ways.
Some days, so far apart, the chasm
left by your passing an endless well
of sorrow. She has been in my life
eighteen years, and I love her
as a daughter. But your death leaves
us uncertain, reaching for one another.

She is moving on with someone new
and my heart breaks for what should
have been. The family I longed for
with you is gone. There are words
of hurt and misunderstanding. I reach
out, knowing I have not been fair
over the years. Using you to speak
for her, not connecting as I should.

We sit across from each other at lunch.
The bare and vulnerable places left
gaping, exposed without you. There
are tears in her eyes when she says
she thinks of you every day. And I share
the crushing emptiness I carry daily.
We remember your larger than life
personality, your opinions on everything,
your logical mind. We agree your hands
were full with the two of us. She tells me,
We are family and always will be.

In a tarot card reading, she is told
you are the ruby cardinal appearing
when least expected. I tell her you are
the sun. Your light so bright some days
it kindles my soul. When I leave,
we embrace. I know you, my beautiful
boy, are guiding us from beyond.

Sanctuary

I tell my friend of the massive
buck, its powerful golden flank and ivory
antlers, standing in my backyard.
She asks, *Were you hallucinating?*
I wonder if I was imagining things,
as I watched the deer in slow motion
sprint across my lawn, glide effortlessly
over my neighbor's fence.

I have often thought my suburban
yard was a sanctuary for wildlife –
its lush grass, hearty shrubs, wild berries.
Sustenance to the opossums and skunks,
who roam after dark. Rats took up
residence last year. A neighbor's
compost pile, bird seed, dog feces,
an endless supply of food.

I read that deer love acorns, apples,
hostas and hydrangeas. As October
approaches, the tomatoes of summer
still tempt. Evergreens not yet dormant,
crimson maple leaves providing nourishment.
Acorn shells are scattered and broken
on the sidewalk by the park. A feast
for any deer family.

I know I'm not hallucinating, after a week
of deep grief. My heart still shattered.
The times I find it hard to breathe
or lift my head to face the morning.
But this day of the deer is real.

You have come before: a white peacock's
flare, the cardinal's noisy song.
Now, you son, the beautiful buck –
my spirit guide, protector.

The Healing

For Kyle

I feel your energy around me –
but little comes through these days.
Not like the first year you were gone,
I found you everywhere. In the sun
on my face, your beacon so bright.

The messages coming when needed
most. On Mother's Day, your voice
in my head: *You can do this Mom.*
I'm okay. I promise. At the library
sale, the book I find with the dedication:
To my son Kyle. There is no greater
happiness than you.

Tonight, I go to the reading looking
for you. An emerald green aura –
its glow bathing me. The psychic
says it's the color of deep healing.
A white peacock – symbol of purity,
cleansing, an illuminated soul.
She sees a pink rose, thorns removed.
Life's beauty stripped of grief.

Then, the words so unexpected –
There is someone on the spirit side
who is proud of you. Your presence
in the room. The peace in knowing
you are watching from the other side.
Proud of the mother I still am.

Legacy

For My Mother

It was a different Christmas this year –
your COPD requiring oxygen full time.
No big holiday meals or wrapped gifts
beneath the tree. No colorful cards.
But you insist my father take you to the mall
to shop. You say, *I want everyone*
to have one gift to open.

I am reminded of your generosity,
so like my grandfather, who gave you soft
cashmere sweaters in pastel colors,
a strand of pearls as Christmas gifts.

But when you leave to spend the winter
in Florida, I fear never seeing you again.
Every trip to the land of sun and endless
beaches, you have bouts of pneumonia.
An illness your lungs won't tolerate now.

So I write you a letter, saying things
I never have. That you are fearless, brave,
and loving. How I cherish all the holidays,
our adventures at the lake, the Sunday dinners.

How we share a bond no one should bear.
Both losing sons, and you a grandson,
me a brother. You showed me how to live
with grief and unimaginable loss and still love.
You taught me what it means to be resilient.

I see my mother with white summer handbag
at her hip, my grandmother with floral knit sweater
draped over shoulders. They are about to leave.
They are beautiful women of strong German stock,
solid, rooted like the oak. They are my legacy.

These Days

For My Father and In Memory
of My Mother (1935-2019)

It's while washing dishes . . .
I see my father bent over
clearing dirt and debris
from my brother's grave marker,
fifty-six years after his death.

It's when I'm walking . . .
I see my father placing flowers:
roses, daisies, blue salvia
in the vase on my mother's
bronze grave marker.
How it glints in the July sun.

It's while making the bed . . .
I see my father wandering
the house, a quiet pall shrouding
the rooms. Sixty-five years
of marriage, her last breath
on a bright May afternoon.
He tells me he sleeps now
on her side of the bed.

It's when taking out the trash . . .
I see my father eating his meals
alone, watching Jeopardy.
His coffee made with K-Cups
now. No need for a full pot.

It's while I feed my dog . . .
I see my father losing weight,
his appetite hijacked by grief.

We shop for new beige khakis,
size 34. Something my mother
would do, telling him to buy
more than one pair.

It's when I brush my teeth . . .
I see my father and the laundry
he now sorts and washes.
Asking for instructions on running
the machines. One Tide pod
and the permanent press setting.

It's while I'm driving . . .
I see my father and myself
forever bonded in the moment.
The hugs, kisses, the whispered
I love you. This void, an empty
vessel unable to be filled.
The bone tired grief we share.

Grandmother Love

For Nell

She will be three on the sixth of March,
and I remember my grandmother passing,
fourteen years ago on the same day.
The circle of life through birth and death.
I am grandmother and granddaughter now.

My grandmother, a painter. Afternoons,
I watched her work in a paint-spattered
blue smock, dipping pencil-thin
brushes into thick oils, marking canvas:
a carriage, church steeple, blonde boy
and his paper boat.

Those same hands soapy at the kitchen
sink, scouring tin foil. Habit from living
through the Depression. The hands
I reached for the last days in the nursing
home, blue-veined and small, asleep
in her lap.

My granddaughter's hands, her long,
slender fingers that roll and pat colorful
Play-Doh shapes, carefully pour tea
into toy cups. Her fingers in prayer position
when we read *Yoga Baby* and try the poses.

I remember her father's hands the day
he was born, big pink fists. The doctor
saying, *These are the hands of an athlete.*
Same hands that cupped her in his palms
the day she was born.

I will see her years from now, in the gym
at his high school, playing volleyball.
Sending the ball soaring across the net.
How proud her father would have been.
The sports he would have coached her in.

I hang a plaque in my bedroom:
I used to think I was too old to fall in love
again but then I became a Grandma.
Every time I see you, sweet Nell,
I fall in love again.

The Little Scientist

For Nell

She asks me if I know what a hypothesis
is? I play along and say no.
She says, *It's when you test an idea.*
I am astounded my four-year-old
granddaughter understands this concept.
But then I think of her mother, grandmother,
great grandfather, all science teachers.
Their attention to the natural world
is her legacy, as she explores downy swans,
the Great Lakes, moss-covered forests.

We visit the Science Center, investigate
the dinosaur lab, unearthing fossils
from prehistoric times. See galaxies
as stargazers in the planetarium. I think
of her father, when I took him walking
through the rock and mineral exhibitions.
Reminders of the luminous stones
and gems he carefully collected. Displayed
with pride alongside his pocketknives,
zippo lighters, baseball cards.

For his daughter's fifth birthday next month,
I buy a new box for her rock collection.
Home to Geodes split open, slices
of yellow amber. The shimmer of Rose
Quartz, Gold Tiger's Eye, Amethyst.
Science in its rustic beauty: Feldspar,
Obsidian, Pumice, Basalt. This gift, perfect
for a new generation. Her father's legacy
bequeathed. The science of his life.

About the Author

Karin Hoffecker has an M.A. in English Literature from Oakland University, Rochester, Michigan. Her poems have appeared in *The Comstock Review*, *The MacGuffin*, *Mona Poetica*, *Passager*, *Peninsula Poets*, and *Penumbra*. Her collection, *The Nell Poems*, was published by Blue Light Press in 2018. She is a retired teacher who enjoys yoga, reading, and spending time with her granddaughter. This collection is written for all those who are here and away. She lives in Birmingham, Michigan.

www.ingramcontent.com/pod-product-compliance
Lightning Source LLC
LaVergne TN
LVHW091321080426

835510LV00007B/599